Patterning Techniques

A pattern is a repetition of shapes and lines that can be simple or complex depending on your preference and the space you want to fill. Even complicated patterns start out very simple with either a line or a shape.

Repeating shapes (floating)

Shapes and lines are the basic building blocks of patterns. Here are some example shapes that we can easily turn into patterns:

Before we turn these shapes into patterns, let's spruce them up a bit by outlining, double-stroking (going over a line more than once to make it thicker), and adding shapes to the inside and outside.

To create a pattern from these embellished shapes, all you have to do is repeat them, as shown below. You can also add small shapes in between the embellished shapes, as shown.

These are called "floating" patterns because they are not attached to a line. These floating patterns can be used to fill space anywhere and can be made big or small, short or long, to suit your needs.

Tip

If you add shapes and patterns to these coloring pages using pens or markers, make sure the ink is completely dry before you color on top of them; otherwise, the ink may smear.

Coloring Techniques & Media

My favorite way to color is to combine a variety of media so I can benefit from the best that each has to offer. When experimenting with new combinations of media, I strongly recommend testing first by layering the colors and media on scrap paper to find out what works and what doesn't. It's a good idea to do all your testing in a sketchbook and label the colors/brands you used for future reference.

Markers & colored pencils

Smooth out areas colored with marker by going over them with colored pencils. Start by coloring lightly, and then apply more pressure if needed.

marker + colored pencil = smoother result

Test your colors on scrap paper first to make sure they match. You don't have to match the colors if you don't want to, though. See the cool effects you can achieve by layering a different color on top of the marker below.

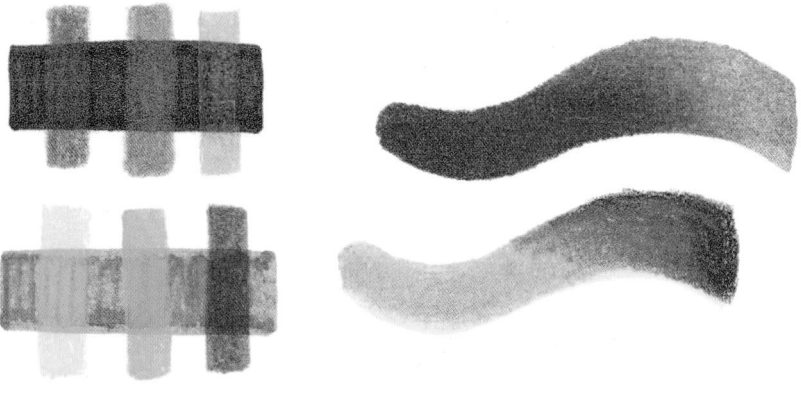

Markers (horizontal) overlapped with colored pencils (vertical).

Purple marker overlapped with white and light blue colored pencils. Yellow marker overlapped with orange and red colored pencils.

Markers & gel pens

Markers and gel pens go hand in hand, because markers can fill large spaces quickly, while gel pens have fine points for adding fun details. White gel pens are especially fun for drawing over dark colors, while glittery gel pens are great for adding sparkly accents.

Color theory

Check out this nifty color wheel. Each color is labeled with a P (primary), S (secondary), or T (tertiary). The **primary colors** are red, yellow, and blue. They are "primary" because they can't be created by mixing other colors. Mixing primary colors creates the **secondary colors** orange, green, and purple (violet). Mixing secondary colors creates the **tertiary colors** yellow-orange, yellow-green, blue-green, blue-purple, red-purple, and red-orange.

Working toward the center of the six large petals, you'll see three rows of lighter colors, called tints. A **tint** is a color plus white. Moving in from the tints, you'll see three rows of darker colors, called shades. A **shade** is a color plus black.

The colors on the top half of the color wheel are considered **warm** colors (red, yellow, orange), and the colors on the bottom half are called **cool** (green, blue, purple).

Colors opposite one another on the color wheel are called **complementary**, and colors that are next to each other are called **analogous**.

Look at the examples and note how each color combo affects the overall appearance and "feel" of the butterfly on the next page. For more inspiration, check out the colored examples on the following pages. Refer to the swatches at the bottom of the page to see the colors selected for each piece.

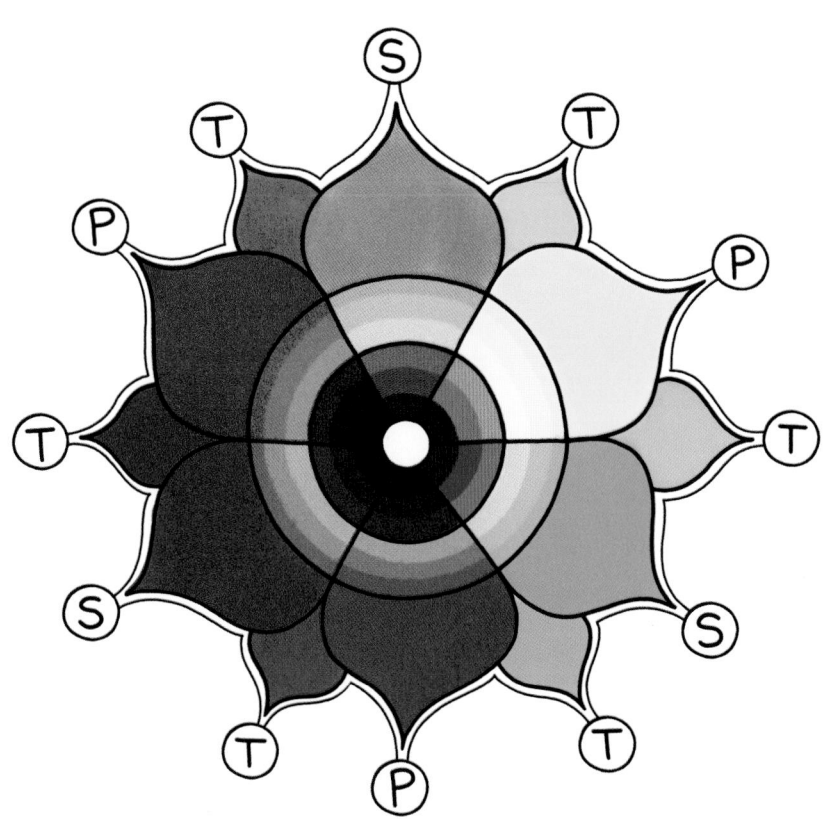

Warm colors

Cool colors

Warm colors with cool accents

Cool colors with warm accents

Tints and shades of red

Tints and shades of blue

Analogous colors

Complementary colors

SYDNEY HARBOUR
AUSTRALIA

Nothing left to do but smile, smile, smile.

—Grateful Dead, *He's Gone*

I want to feel as free as the flowers.

—Unknown

HAPPY DAY

PEACE

You belong somewhere you feel free.

—Tom Petty, *Wildflowers*

You're braver than you believe, stronger than you seem, and smarter than you think.

—A. A. Milne, *Winnie-the-Pooh*

Dala Horse and Kurbits, Sweden.
The Dala horse is the national toy of Sweden and, according to legend, King Charles XII had them carved as gifts for guests.

If your hair is done properly and you're wearing good shoes, you can get away with anything.

—Iris Apfel

Certainly, travel is more than the seeing of sights;
it is a change that goes on, deep and permanent,
in the ideas of living.

—Miriam Beard

Sydney Harbour, Australia.
Located along Sydney Harbour, the Sydney Opera House
features curved triangular architectural
details representative of ship sails.

Why change? Everyone has his own style.
When you have found it, you should stick to it.

—Audrey Hepburn

For whatever we lose (like a you or a me),
It's always our self we find in the sea.

—e. e. cummings

The mountains are calling and I must go.

—John Muir

Being happy never goes out of style.

—Lilly Pulitzer

Be yourself. Everyone else is already taken.

—Oscar Wilde

Hold hands, not grudges.

—Unknown

I feel good, in a special way
I'm in love and it's a sunny day
Good day sunshine

—The Beatles, *Good Day Sunshine*

You can dance, you can jive,
having the time of your life.
See that girl, watch that scene,
digging the Dancing Queen.

—ABBA, *Dancing Queen*

It's what's inside that counts.

—Unknown

Matryoshka Doll, Russia.
The very first Russian nesting doll was taken to the 1900 World's Fair in Paris, France, where it won a bronze medal in the toy division of the competition.

If you want something you've never had,
then you've got to do something
you've never done.

—Unknown

Be yourself.
An original is always worth more than a copy.

—Unknown

Music expresses that which cannot be put
into words and that which cannot remain silent.

—Victor Hugo

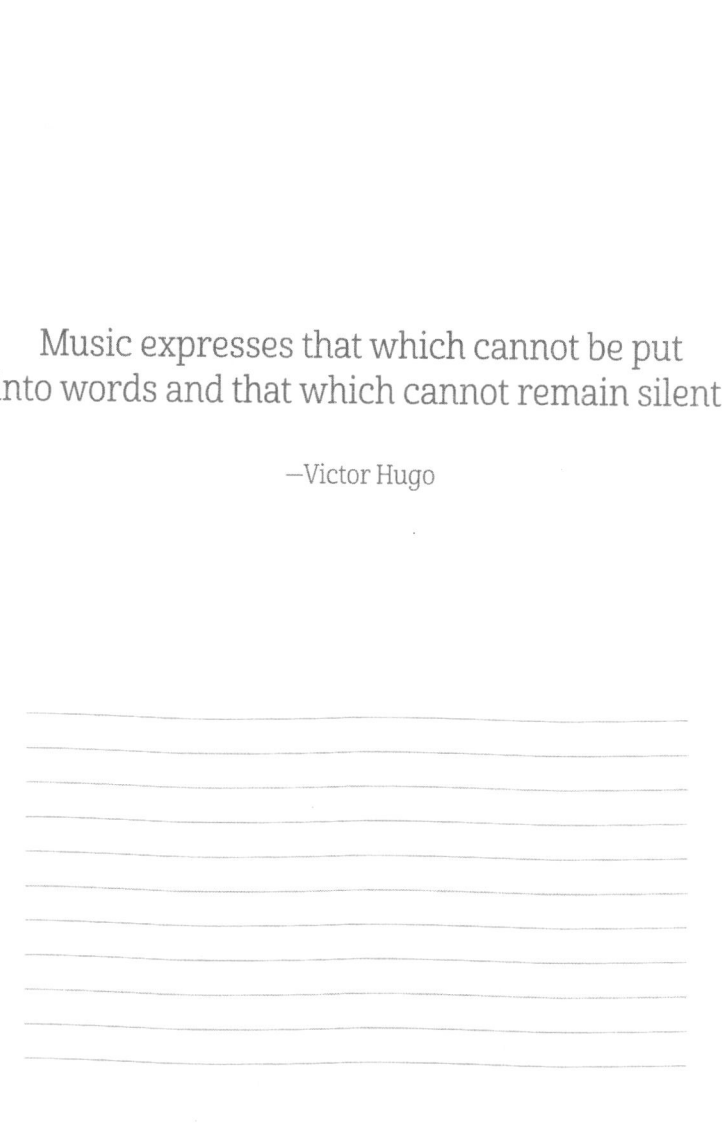

All good things are wild and free.

—Henry David Thoreau

On matters of style, swim with the current,
on matters of principle, stand like a rock.

—Thomas Jefferson

When I die, sprinkle my ashes over the '80s.

—David Lee Roth of Van Halen

A smile is a curve that sets everything straight.

—Phyllis Diller

Kokeshi Doll, Japan.
You may recognize the basic look and feel of the Japanese kokeshi doll when playing your Nintendo Wii—the Mii characters you create are inspired by these dolls.

Work like you don't need the money.
Love like you've never been hurt.
Dance like nobody's watching.

—Satchel Paige

One creates oneself.

—Grace Jones

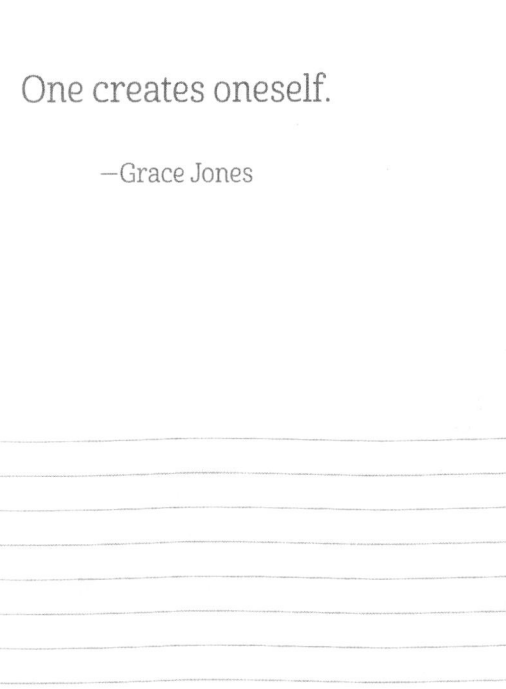

It's the Circle of Life
And it moves us all
Through despair and hope
Through faith and love
'Til we find our place
On the path unwinding
in the Circle, the Circle of Life

—Elton John, *The Circle of Life*

Blessed are the curious, for they
shall have adventures.

—Lovelle Drachman

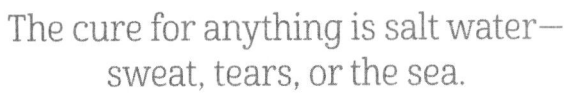

The cure for anything is salt water—
sweat, tears, or the sea.

—Isak Dinesen

The best way to predict the future is to create it.

—Unknown